Table of Contents

Contents

Message from the President of the United States

"After almost eight years as your President, I have been so privileged to learn from you and spend time with many of you while visiting more Tribal communities than any other President. Because I pledged to all of you when I first ran for President that I'd be a partner with all of you in the spirit of a true nation-to-nation relationship, to give all our children the future they deserve. And by creating the White House Council of Native American Affairs, we created a permanent institution with a long-term, Cabinet-level focus on Indian Country, one that involves you through the decision-making process."

- *President Barack Obama, September 29, 2016 White House Tribal Nations Conference.*

President Barack Obama being honored with a blanket ceremony and song during the 8th White House Tribal Nations Conference in Washington, D.C., September 29, 2016.

Executive Summary

Historic progress has been made during the Obama Administration to improve the nation-to-nation relationship between the United States and federally recognized Tribes. The Obama Administration and Tribal Nations have worked together to accomplish shared goals and achieve milestones that upheld self-governance and self-determination – the foundation for prosperous and resilient Tribal nations.

President Obama created a new tradition by inviting elected Tribal leaders from each of the now 567 federally-recognized Indian Tribes across the country to attend the annual White House Tribal Nations Conference. Each year during his Administration, the President and his Cabinet officials met with Tribes to discuss Tribal priorities and to chart the next course of action to address the many needs across Indian Country.

While the Administration and Tribes have partnered for historic achievements, there is still much more to do. President Obama signed Executive Order 13647 on June 26, 2013, establishing the White House Council on Native American Affairs (WHCNAA). The WHCNAA represents a path to a more effective federal government for Indian Country, bringing together federal Departments and Agencies from across the Executive Branch to "break down siloes" and coordinate for more effective programs.

This report outlines some of the shared successes of this Administration while working alongside Tribes. The report intends to set a baseline of progress for Tribal nations to reference in their ongoing work with the federal government. This report highlights what functioned well and what still needs more attention. The report also shares priorities that the WHCNAA will continue to work on as a result of Tribal leaders' recommendations. As demonstrated over the past eight years, when Tribal nations and the federal government work together in a true spirt of nation-to-nation cooperation, a momentous level of progress is achievable. Moving forward, strong leadership from Tribal nations will be critical in ensuring that the progress made over the past eight years builds momentum for continued progress for many Administrations to come.

Improving the Nation-to-Nation Relationship

Over the past eight years, the Administration has strengthened the nation-to-nation relationship by striving to uphold the federal government's treaty and trust responsibilities to Tribal nations. Long-standing, historic disputes with Tribes and American Indians and Alaska Natives were settled during the Obama Administration, facilitating the opportunity for Tribes and the federal government to move beyond the tension and cost of protracted litigation. Those settlements have infused billions of dollars into Indian Country, creating opportunities for economic development, social services, and Tribal government programs. In addition, hundreds of thousands of acres of Tribal homelands have been restored in trust for Tribes. Some additional highlights include:

- **Creating the White House Council on Native American Affairs.** A more efficient federal government has emerged through improved coordination and collaboration among federal agencies and with Tribal nations. The formation of the White House Council on Native American Affairs (WHCNAA), which is chaired by the Secretary of the Interior, coordinates inter-agency staff, programs, and expertise across the Executive Branch. While WHCNAA membership consists of heads of Departments and Agencies, engaging Tribal leaders in the WHCNAA has been key to creating effective policies and programs that positively affect Tribes.

- **Prioritizing Tribal Consultation**. Tribal consultation has been reinforced during this Administration as a priority and important step in the federal decision making process. Incorporating and considering Tribal perspectives into the decision-making process when federal agency actions have an impact on Tribal interests, leads to the more effective implementation of federal programs, policies, and regulations. President Obama reaffirmed the federal commitment to Tribal consultation through Presidential Memorandum on November 5, 2009, continuing the commitment expressed by President George W. Bush in his Presidential Memorandum on September 23, 2004, and President William J. Clinton's Executive Order 13175 on November 6, 2000. A number of federal agencies have implemented their own consultations policies, ensuring regular communication with Tribes on matters directly impacting Tribal affairs. For all the progress made, how federal agencies approach and implement Tribal consultation varies considerably from agency to agency an area where the WHCNAA and federal agencies should put energy and focus in the years to come.

- **Land Buy-Back Program for Tribal Nations.** Through the Department of the Interior's Land Buy-Back Program for Tribal Nations (Buy-Back Program), authorized by the historic Cobell Settlement achieved in 2009, the Obama administration worked closely with Tribal governments to provide Indian landowners with the voluntary opportunity to consolidate fractional land interests. The Program provided $1.9 billion to purchase fractional interests at fair market value within 10 years. Since the Program began making offers in December 2013, more than $925 million has been paid to individual landowners and the equivalent of almost 1.7 million acres of land has been restored to Tribal governments. Returning fractionated lands to Tribes in trust has enormous potential to improve Tribal community resources by increasing home site locations, improving transportation routes, spurring Tribal economic development, and preserving traditional cultural or ceremonial sites.

  The Program has announced an implementation schedule of 105 locations, which includes more than 96 percent of all landowners with fractional interests and more than 98 percent of both fractional interests and equivalent acres in Program-eligible areas. Thus far, the Department has entered into agreements with 40 Tribal nations to cooperatively implement the Buy-Back Program.

- **Settling Historic Disputes.** Since January 2009, the United States settled the trust accounting and trust mismanagement claims of 104 Tribes for $3.35 billion, resulting in the resolution of 69 lawsuits without the need for protracted litigation. The Department of the Interior (DOI) manages about 2,500 Tribal trust accounts for more than 250 federally recognized Tribes. In addition, it manages almost 56 million acres of Tribal trust lands and more than 100,000 leases on those lands for various uses, including housing, timber harvesting, farming, grazing, oil and gas extraction, business leasing, rights-of-way and easements.

  In announcing the settlements with 17 Tribes for almost $493 million in September 2016, Attorney General Lynch noted that "[t]hese historical grievances were a barrier to our shared progress toward a brighter future," but that with the settlements "those barriers have been removed and decades of contention have been ended honorably and fairly."

  Over the last eight years, the Obama Administration has completed and enacted more water Indian rights settlements than any previous administration. DOI and the Department of Justice (DOJ) contributed to 12 landmark Indian water rights settlements and corresponding statutes which, when fully implemented, will resolve complex and contentious water rights issues in New Mexico, Arizona, Montana, California, Idaho and Nevada. The total funding authorized for these settlements is close to $3 billion, an enormous commitment that will improve the quality of life for Tribal members on several Indian reservations by bringing critical infrastructure to provide safe drinking water and support economic development activities, such as the development of hydroelectric power, agriculture improvements, and water marketing. Additionally, DOJ intervened in a case in support of the Agua Caliente Band of Cahuilla Indians and successfully argued that the Tribe's federal reserved water rights may include groundwater. Further, DOJ contributed to six landmark Indian water rights settlements and corresponding statutes which, when fully implemented, will resolve complex and contentious water rights issues in New Mexico, Arizona, Montana and Nevada. DOJ also successfully defended claims for the benefit of the Klamath Tribes in the Klamath Basin Adjudication in Oregon; for the Confederated Tribes of the Yakama Nation in the Yakima River Basin in Washington; and the Pyramid Lake Paiute Tribe in Nevada. DOJ remains involved in 29 complex water rights adjudications in nearly every western state.

- **Defending Reservation Boundaries.** DOJ helped obtain important court victories that support Tribal boundaries and Tribal jurisdiction over Tribal lands. For example, DOJ supported the Omaha Tribe in Tribal court, U.S. district court, the Eighth Circuit Court of Appeals, and the Supreme Court, successfully arguing that the Omaha Reservation remained intact and had not been diminished by 1882 legislation authorizing the sale of land on the western edge of the reservation. In March 2016, the Supreme Court confirmed its prior holdings that only Congress can diminish a reservation, and held that the 1882 legislation did not do so. DOJ also helped the Saginaw Chippewa Indian Tribe establish the existence and boundaries of its reservation through a 2010 settlement between the Tribe, the United States, the State of Michigan and local governments, which included a series of landmark intergovernmental agreements that provide much-needed clarity regarding authority over law enforcement, child welfare, taxation and land use matters. In addition, DOJ successfully supported the existence of the Yankton Sioux Reservation in South Dakota by defeating claims that the reservation had been disestablished.

- **Restoring Tribal Homelands.** Since 2009, the Bureau of Indian Affairs within DOI has processed 2,265 trust applications and restored more than 542,000 acres of Tribal homeland into trust. The Administration has overhauled antiquated leasing regulations to provide Tribes greater control over their homelands and issued new regulations to allow DOI to accept land into trust for federally recognized Alaska Tribes, thereby advancing Tribal sovereignty and closing a long-standing gap that had not extended this eligibility to Alaska Natives.

DOI and DOJ have worked to address the Supreme Court's 2009 decision in *Carcieri v. Salazar*, which held that DOI could not take land into trust for Tribes that had not been "under federal jurisdiction" when the Indian Reorganization Act was enacted in 1934. Interior, in its budget requests, has transmitted to Congress language that would fix the resulting impact on Interior's ability to take land into trust in those circumstances. Pending adoption of that fix, DOI has developed a framework to determine whether a tribe was "under federal jurisdiction" at that time, thus addressing the uncertainty created by the *Carcieri* decision and allowing Interior to address the backlog of trust applications that developed in the wake of that decision.

Since then, DOJ has successfully defended DOI's decisions to take land into trust under the new post-Carcieri framework. In July 2016, the D.C. Circuit Court of Appeals upheld the framework, as well as Interior's decision to acquire land into trust for the Cowlitz Indian Tribe based on a determination that the Tribe was "under federal jurisdiction" in 1934. In another case, *Poarch Band of Creek Indians v. Hildreth*, the United States supported the tribe's efforts to prevent unlawful taxation of Tribal property, arguing that the tax assessor could not indirectly challenge land-into-trust acquisition through the guise of a tax-collection action when it did not challenge the acquisition directly. DOJ also filed an amicus brief in the Ninth Circuit in *Big Lagoon Rancheria v. California*, arguing that California was improperly attacking DOI's 1994 decision to take the land into trust, as well as its decision to recognize the Rancheria as a tribe. The Ninth Circuit agreed with the position in the United States' brief. DOJ has also successfully defended challenges to Interior decisions accepting parcels of land in trust for three Indian Tribes in California.

- **Providing a Process for Reestablishing a Government-to-Government Relationship with Native Hawaiians.** DOI promulgated a final rule that provides an administrative mechanism for reestablishing a government-to-government relationship between the United States and the Native Hawaiian community. Native Hawaiians are the largest indigenous group in the United States that lacks a government-to-government relationship with the United States. The rule would leave it to the Native Hawaiian community to decide whether to form a government, and to determine whether to seek a government-to-government relationship with the United States.

- **Improving Tribal and Native Hawaiian Involvement in the National Historic Preservation Program.** In celebration of the 50th anniversary of the National Historic Preservation Act (NHPA), early in 2016 the Advisory Council on Historic Preservation (ACHP) launched an effort to improve the effectiveness of the national historic preservation program. The ACHP is developing a set of policy recommendations and achievable implementation strategies that can be implemented through legislative, executive, or administrative action. Since the NHPA provides Indian Tribes a critical opportunity to have a voice in federal decision making about projects that might affect

Tribal sacred and historic places, the ACHP sought input from Tribal leaders and preservation staff as well as intertribal organizations about ways to improve Tribal involvement in the national historic preservation program. Their responses are included in the recommendations and will be formally submitted to the next Administration and the incoming Congress at the end of this year. They will also provide direction for the ACHP's Office of Native American Affairs.

- **Secretarial & Departmental Tribal Advisory Groups.** The Department of Health and Human Services (HHS) established the first ever Cabinet level Tribal Advisory Committee, the Secretary's Tribal Advisory Committee (STAC) to create a coordinated, department-wide strategy to incorporate Tribal guidance on HHS priorities, policies and budget, improve the Government-to-Government relationship, and mechanisms for continuous improvement with our partnership with Indian Tribes. The Administration for Children and Families and the National Institutes for Health within HHS also established Tribal Advisory Committees to continue the tradition of supporting Tribal consultation activities across the Department. In addition to the STAC, HHS has six Tribal Advisory Committees to serve divisions within HHS.

  The U.S. Department of Agriculture (USDA) created the Council for Native American Farming and Ranching (CNAFR) in 2012. Originally established pursuant to the Keepseagle settlement, the CNAFR has been re-established to advise the USDA Secretary on ways to eliminate barriers to participation for Native American Farmers and Ranchers in USDA programs.

  The Department of Treasury announced in 2015 appointments to serve on its Tribal Advisory Committee (TTAC). The TTAC advise the Secretary on matter related to the taxation of Indians, the training of Internal Revenue Service field agents, and the provision of training and technical assistance to Native American financial officers. The TTAC was established in keeping with the Tribal General Welfare Exclusion Act of 2014. TTAC committee members are appointed but the Chairs and Ranking Members of the Senate Finance Committee, and the House of Representatives Ways and Means Committee. Each Committee Chair or Ranking Member will appoint one TTAC member.

  DOJ established a Tribal Nations Leadership Council (TNLC), composed of Tribal leaders selected by the Tribes themselves and charged with advising the Attorney General on issues critical to Tribal governments and communities. The TNLC has met regularly since late 2010 with the Attorney General and other DOJ senior leaders.

- **Tribal Treaty Rights.** On February 19, 2016, the Environmental Protection Agency (EPA) issued a Guidance for Discussion Tribal Treaty Rights (Guidance) as an adjunct to the EPA Policy on Consultation and Coordination with Indian Tribes (2011). The Guidance is designed to enhance EPA's consultation efforts in situations where Tribal treaty rights relating to natural resources may exist in a specific geographic area that is the focus of a proposed EPA action. EPA developed the Guidance after extensive national consultation with Tribes and making the decision to issue a clear statement regarding the role of Tribal treaty rights 30 years after issuing the EPA Policy for the Administration of Environmental Programs on Indian Reservations.

- **Tribal Treaty Rights MOU.** Additionally, the agency members of the interagency Environment, Climate Change, and Natural Resources Subgroup of the WHCNAA entered into a Memorandum of Understanding (MOU) in the fall of 2016 to improve how agencies integrate consideration of Tribal treaty and similar rights on natural resources into agency decision-making processes. As of December 2016 signatories include, the Departments of Agriculture, Commerce, Defense, Interior, Justice and Transportation, the Environmental Protection Agency, as well as the White House Council on Environmental Quality and the Advisory Council on Historic Preservation. A total of nine Departments, Agencies, and Councils had signed onto the MOU, affirming the federal government's legal responsibility to protect Tribal treaty rights and similar Tribal rights, especially those that concern the use of natural resources.

Also in 2016, DOJ and DOI, working with Pacific Northwest Tribes, obtained a significant victory in the Ninth Circuit Court of Appeals in *United States v. Washington*, which confirmed the habitat component of the treaty fishing right. The Ninth Circuit decision specifically affirmed that the State of Washington's construction and maintenance of highway and railroad culverts impeded the migration of salmon to and from spawning grounds in violation of the treaty fishing right. The decision affirmed that the State must reconfigure these culverts which have resulted in the dramatic reduction of salmon available for treaty harvest over the last 30 years.

- **U.S. Fish and Wildlife Service Native American Policy Update Companion Policy.** In 2016, the U.S. Fish and Wildlife Service (USFWS) within the DOI updated and revised its Native American Policy and how it is implemented. Additionally, the Alaska Region of the USFWS is developing a companion step-down policy for its many unique mandates and relationship to Alaska Native people.

- **USDA Department-Wide Regulations on Consultation.** USDA published its current Departmental Regulations on Tribal Consultation, Coordination, and Collaboration

(DR1305-002). These regulations establish over-arching Department-wide guidance for all USDA agencies, providing a baseline from which individual agencies develop and refine their own specific, supplemental Tribal consultation policies.

- **National Park Service Rule for Tribes on Plant Gathering.** In 2016, the National Park Service within DOI changed a regulation (26 CFR Part 2) to allow citizens of federally recognized Tribes traditionally associated with parks to gather plants or plant parts for traditional uses on lands within areas of the National Park System where those practices traditionally occurred, without causing a significant adverse impact to park resources or values.

- **Department of Justice Principles for Working with Federally Recognized Tribes.** In 2014, the Attorney General issued principles for DOJ in working with federally recognized Tribes. The principles are intended to improve the internal management of DOJ and honor the government-to-government relationship between the United States and each federally recognized tribe.

- **Aid for Disaster Relief.** In 2013, the Robert T. Stafford Disaster Relief and Emergency Assistance Act (Stafford Act) authorized the President to make certain programs of assistance available to supplement Tribal, state, territorial, and local efforts to respond to and recover from an incident that exceeds all available resources and overwhelms the Tribal, state, territorial, and local governments. On January 29, 2013, the President strengthened the relationship of the Federal Emergency Management Agency (FEMA) within the Department of Homeland Security with Tribal governments by signing the Sandy Recovery Improvement Act of 2013 (SRIA). SRIA amended the Stafford Act to provide Federally-recognized Tribal governments the option to request a Presidential emergency or major disaster declaration independent of a state.

- **Protecting Voting Rights of American Indian and Alaska Natives.** On June 9, 2014, then-Attorney General Holder criticized election practices that adversely affect the ability of American Indian and Alaska Native populations to exercise their right to vote, including inaccessible polling places in Tribal areas, English-only ballots for areas with limited English proficiency and "precinct realignment" practices that attempt to combine geographically isolated Native communities.

On May 21, 2015, the department formally proposed legislation that would require states or localities whose territory includes part or all of an Indian reservation, an Alaska Native village, or other Tribal lands to locate at least one polling place in a venue selected by the Tribal government. The Department's Civil Rights Division has been active in enforcing

11

the voting rights of Native Americans, including the right to vote without discrimination and the right, in some jurisdictions, to have voter information available in certain Native languages. Since 2009, the division has enforced Native American voting rights in Alaska, Arizona, Mississippi, New Mexico and South Dakota

Consultation

The concept of Tribal consultation arises from the unique legal and political relationship between the federal government and Tribal nations, a relationship grounded in the U.S. Constitution, treaties, statutes, executive orders and judicial decisions. Departments and agencies strengthened their consultation policies and efforts in response to President Obama's Memorandum signed at the first Tribal Nations Conference in 2009 directing Federal agencies to submit detailed plans of actions on how they intend to secure regular and meaningful consultation and collaboration with Tribal officials in the development of Federal policies that have Tribal implications, pursuant to Executive Order 13175. Some highlights include:

- **The White House Tribal Nations Conference.** In 2009, Administration officials and Tribal leaders pledged to work together to engage in meaningful consultation that respects the sovereignty of Tribes and the right of Tribes to self-governance. This pledge was memorialized by a Presidential Memorandum signed at the first Tribal Nations Conference. The President held a Tribal Nations Conference every year of his Administration.

- **Principles for Working with Federally Recognized Indian Tribes.** In 2016, the Administration for Children and Families (ACF) within the Department of Health and Human Services (HHS) established *Principles for Working with Federally Recognized Indian Tribes,* a policy standard governing ACF's relationships with federally recognized Indian Tribes. The Principles are designed to extend and complement ACF's Tribal Consultation Policy and to articulate ACF's commitment to promote and sustain strong government-to-government relationships, foster Indian self-determination, protect Tribal sovereignty, and to demonstrate accountability for and transparency in ACF's actions as public servants.

- **Refining Expanding and Engaging in Tribal Consultation.** In 2016, the Department of Housing and Urban Development (HUD) published its revised Tribal consultation policy, proposed a Tribal advisory committee to further develop and improve its Indian housing programs through enhanced government-to-government communications, and completed three years of negotiated rulemaking that resulted in a new Indian Housing Block Grant Formula Final Rule.

- **Improving Tribal and Native Hawaiian consultation in federal project planning.** In response to the issuance of the Presidential Memorandum on Tribal Consultation and building on the Advisory Council Historic Preservation's (ACHP) longstanding efforts, the ACHP issued an unprecedented amount of guidance on topics ranging from the integration of Section 106 and the U.N. Declaration on the Rights of Indigenous Peoples to the role of applicants in federal-Tribal consultation. The ACHP also published Recommendations for Improving Tribal-Federal Consultation.

- **Protection of Confidential Information.** The ACHP issued a "Frequently Asked Questions" guidance document on protecting sensitive information about historic properties under Section 304 of the National Historic Preservation Act. Federal agency officials, SHPOs, THPOs, Indian Tribes, Native Hawaiian organizations, and other stakeholders in the Section 106 process often ask ACHP staff how sensitive information about historic properties can be protected from public disclosure.

- **The Rail Safety Improvement Act of 2008.** The Railway Safety Improvement Act of 2008 mandated that positive train control wireless public safety systems be deployed across most of the country's rail network by December 31, 2015. In order to meet this mandate, railroad companies have been installing more than 20,000 communications poles in railroad rights-of-way, including rights-of-way on Tribal lands. During the safety system deployment the Federal Communications Commission, in coordination with the ACHP worked to ensure that the railroad companies complied with the National Historic Preservation Act, which requires federal agencies to consult with Tribes to avoid or minimize impacts of federal actions on sites of religious and cultural significance to Tribal nations.

- **Consultation with Tribes on Environment Issues.** On May 4, 2011, the Environmental Protection Agency (EPA) finalized its Policy on Consultation and Coordination with Indian Tribes after extensive collaboration with Tribes and a public comment period. The Policy establishes a broader standard regarding the type of Agency actions and activities that may warrant consultation. This broader standard is drawn from EPA's 1984 Indian Policy, which states that "Tribal concerns and interests are considered whenever EPA's actions and/or decisions may affect" Tribes. During the first six months of the new Policy being in effect, nearly 120 Agency consultations were planned or underway.

- **Infrastructure and Infrastructure-Related Projects.** In the fall of 2016, several federal agencies with the Departments of Interior, Justice, and the Army at the helm, committed to a broad review and consultation with Tribes on how Federal decision-making on infrastructure and related projects can better allow for timely and meaningful input from Tribes. While each Tribe's comments were unique to their respective experiences, Tribes spoke with one voice as to the need for improvement in how and when Federal agencies engage Tribes prior to authorizing or otherwise initiating Federal infrastructure decisions. Agencies will publish a report on the findings of this consultation along with recommended agency actions in January 2017.

Education and Native Youth

A cornerstone of the Administration's efforts with Indian Country has been its work with Native youth. The commitment to Native youth has been embraced by a broad array of federal agencies who undertook initiatives ranging from direct engagement to program development and agency reforms. Highlights include:

- **Generation Indigenous (Gen-I).** Gen-I is an inter-agency, all of government initiative seeking to improve the lives of Native youth through new investments and increased engagement. Gen-I improves the lives of Native youth by promoting a national dialogue and policies and programs to mobilize and cultivate the next generation of Native leaders. Thousands of Native youth and organizations have accepted the Gen-I challenge by joining the Native Youth Network to give back in a positive way to their communities. Together in partnership with the federal government, Gen-I is building a nationwide commitment to ensure that our Native youth have the tools they need to thrive.

- **White House Tribal Youth Gatherings.** In an effort to elevate young Native American youth issues and to promote dialogue between the highest level of federal leadership and Native youth leaders, the White Youth Tribal Youth Gatherings were created. The first Youth Gathering was held in Washington, DC, during the summer of 2015, with thousands of youth from across the country attending. The second Tribal Youth Gathering was held in conjunction with the 2016 White House Tribal Nations Conference.

- **National Intertribal Youth Summit.** Starting with a 2013 grant award, the Department of Justice (DOJ) launched the National Intertribal Youth Leadership Development Initiative, now known as Today's Native Leaders (TNL), which consists of youth gatherings, opportunities, and services to develop leadership skills among cohorts of Tribal youth. In Fiscal Year 2016, TNL held regional gatherings in Spokane, WA (Winter 2015), Minneapolis, MN (Spring 2016) and Anchorage, AK (September 2016). The gatherings were co-facilitated by Native youth leaders and enabled participants to design community service projects related to anti-bullying, culture camps, documentary projects, organizing conferences for Native youth, and developing wellness and other activities that serve as alternatives to alcohol and substance use for youth. In addition, TNL held three webinars covering the following topics: "Getting the Right Attention: Developing a Communications Plan for Your Youth Council," "How to Create a Year-Long Calendar for Your Youth Council," and "How to Create a More Inclusive Environment in Your Youth Program for LGTBQ 2-SpiritYouth." Hundreds of Native youth completed each of these programs.

- **Native Youth Metrics Work Group.** The White House Council for Native American Affairs (WHCNAA) and the Office of Management and Budget created a Native Youth Metrics Work Group among several federal agencies. These federal agencies have been working together to establish metrics to measure their progress in the following priority areas: improving educational and life outcomes at Bureau of Indian Education (BIE) schools, increasing access to quality teacher housing, improved access to the internet, supporting the implementation of the Indian Child Welfare Act (ICWA), reducing teen suicide, and increasing Tribal control of criminal justice. This inter-agency effort to establish metrics and collect data is critical to ensuring federal agencies are held accountable to the United States' trust responsibly and ensuring federal investments in Indian Country are improving the lives and opportunities for Native Youth.

- **Safeguarding the Rights of Indian Children and Families**. The Departments of the Interior (DOI), HHS, and DOJ have made significant strides to promote implementation and compliance with the Indian Child Welfare Act (ICWA), an important federal law designed to maintain Indian children with their families and Tribes. The agencies formalized this cooperation in a Memorandum of Understanding signed in April 2016.

In June 2016, DOI issued regulations that will improve compliance with ICWA and promote nationwide consistency in Indian child-welfare proceedings, and has also issued updated guidelines that assist state courts and agencies in implementing the statute and regulations. DOJ has filed amicus briefs in state and federal courts, helping to bring about decisions that are faithful to the letter and the spirit of the Indian Child Welfare Act. This year, DOJ obtained two favorable rulings from the California Supreme Court. DOJ also successfully defended a challenge to Interior's ICWA guidelines in federal district court.

- **Advisory Council on Historic Preservation Native Youth Strategic Plan.** In response to the President's announcement about Generation Indigenous, in 2015, the Advisory Council on Historic Preservation (ACHP) adopted the Native Youth Strategic Plan. Under the plan, the ACHP launched a Facebook page for Native youth called Preservation Indigenous-Native Youth, developed a partnership with Salish Kootenai College's Tribal Historic Preservation Program, and hosted several preservation events around the county. In 2016, the ACHP sought input from Tribal leaders and preservation staff on their priorities and how best to reach out to Native youth. Based on this input, the ACHP produced an initial set of historic preservation information geared for both Native youth and adults working with them. The information is intended to introduce Native youth to historic preservation, in general, and as a potential career path. It is available online and was sent to Tribal leaders, inter-Tribal organizations, and Tribal preservation staff.

  The ACHP established an interagency working group focused on expanding existing and creating new federal programs to introduce Native youth to historic preservation both as a way to participate in the protection of sacred places and as a potential career path. Members of the working group include the DOI's Bureau of Indian Affairs, the National Park Service, the Bureau of Ocean Energy Management, and the Bureau of Reclamation, along with USDA's U.S. Forest Service, and the Repatriation Office of the National Museum of Natural History.

- **Bureau of Indian Education Reform**. In 2013, Secretary of the Interior, Sally Jewell, and Secretary of Education, Arne Duncan, convened an American Indian Education Study Group to diagnose the systemic challenges facing DOI's Bureau of Indian Education (BIE) and to propose a comprehensive plan for reform to ensure all students attending BIE-funded schools receive a world-class education.

  The Study Group drafted a framework for reform based on several listening sessions last fall with Tribal leaders, Indian educators and others throughout Indian Country on how to facilitate Tribal sovereignty in American Indian education and how to improve educational outcomes for students at BIE-funded schools. The Study Group met with nearly 400 individuals and received nearly 200 comments. Based on that input, the Study Group prepared a draft framework for educational reform that became the subject of four Tribal consultation sessions held in April and May of 2014. The Study Group incorporated feedback it received from Tribal leaders and other BIE stakeholders into the final Blueprint for Reform, released on June 13, 2014.

  The Blueprint for Reform sets as its goals to improve academic and life outcomes for the BIE's students, and to increase Tribal sovereignty in education. In February 2016,

Congress lifted its final reservations on implementing the Blueprint, allowing the BIE and DOI to begin implementation. Phase I involved the realignment of the internal organization of BIE from a regional basis to a structure based on the types of schools serviced; namely, (1) schools in the Navajo Nation, (2) Tribally-controlled schools, and (3) BIE-operated schools. Phase I also replaced the Line Offices with Educational Resource Centers ("ERCs") which will house School Solutions Teams. BIE began implementing Phase I of the reorganization in early 2016 after Congress issued a "notice of no objection" to the BIE. Phase I is nearing completion. To date 53% of BIE's restructured positions have been filled, including critical positions designed to increase services to students, such as the Student Health Program Specialist. In addition, BIE is expeditiously moving forward to fill all remaining vacant positions. BIE plans to begin implementing Phase II of the reorganization sometime in 2017.

The BIE launched the Sovereignty in Indian Education (SIE) Enhancement Initiative and administered the Tribal Education Department (TED) Grant program. The purpose of SIE is to equip Tribes with the necessary tools to take control of BIE-operated schools that serve their Tribal members. The TED program is specifically funded by Congress and further assists Tribal education departments in the planning and coordinating all educational programs. The bulk of TED grantees have utilized their funds to develop Tribal educational codes. To date the BIE has awarded ten (10) TED grants and eight (8) SIE grants. BIE projects that by the close of school year 2017-2018 more than $8 million will have been invested into Tribal educational reform and Tribal capacity initiatives. Since 2013 BIE has successfully transferred five (5) BIE-operated schools to Tribal control and operation.

- **White House Initiative on American Indian and Alaska Native Education**. Since its creation in 2011, the White House Initiative on American Indian and Alaska Native Education has taken a number of significant steps to implement Executive Order (EO) 13592, *Improving American Indian and Alaska Native Education Opportunities and Strengthening Tribal Colleges and Universities*. As part of implementing this EO, the Departments of Education (ED) and DOI, created a Committee on Indian Education, which includes Tribal leader representatives from the Tribal Interior Budget Council. This committee leverages the expertise of each department to implement seven goals and specific activities of a 2012 DOI-ED Memorandum of Understanding. The group first met in February 2013 and continues to meet regularly, bringing together Senior Administration Officials from as many as 29 federal agencies and offices to focus on expanding educational opportunities and improving outcomes for AI/AN students, including helping to ensure that AI/AN students have an opportunity to learn their native Languages.

- **Revitalization and Preservation of Native Languages.** In October 2016, the Administration for Native Americans (ANA) within HHS, the BIE at DOI, and the White House Initiative on American Indian and Alaska Native Education (WHIAIANE) housed at the Department of Education (ED), hosted the Interagency Native American Languages Summit. In September 2015, ED, HHS-ANA and DOI-BIE hosted a second Native Languages Summit to identify best practices in preserving and revitalizing Native languages. In November 2012, the agencies signed a Memorandum of Agreement to collaborate on programming, resource development and policy initiatives across the government. The first Language summit was held in June 2014 bringing together 300 participants from across the country. As a part of this work, BIE has developed a Native Language Policy Framework for BIE-funded schools.

- **Grant Support for Native Youth.** In 2016, the Administration for Native Americans (ANA) within the Department of Health and Human Services awarded nearly $3 million in funds under two new grant programs to support Native youth, Native Language Community Coordination Demonstration Projects (NLCC) and Native Youth Initiative for Leadership, Empowerment, and Development (I-LEAD). The NLCC furthers the vision of ANA's Native Languages Preservation and Maintenance Program supporting site-based educational programs to demonstrate evidence based strategies that integrate Native language and educational services within a specific community. The I-LEAD program supports local community projects that foster Native youth resiliency, and empower Native youth across four broad domains of activity: (1) Native youth leading (leadership development), (2) Native youth connecting (building positive identity, community connection, and social-emotional health), (3) Native youth learning (educational success), and (4) Native youth working (workforce readiness).

- **Enhancing Support for Climate & Environment Education for Native Youth.** In 2015 and 2016, U.S. Fish and Wildlife Service, Bureau of Indian Affairs (BIA), the National Park Service (NPS), U.S. Geological Survey (USGS), at the Department of Interior along with the Environmental Protection Agency, National Oceanic and Atmospheric Administration, and U.S. Department of Agriculture's (USDA) Forest Service hosted the first two Inter-Tribal Youth Climate Leadership Congress (Congress) to promote youth engagement and positive community action for climate resilience. Participating Native American, Alaska Native, and Native Hawaiian students learned about climate change issues in indigenous communities, federal agency efforts to address impacts, and how the students can help their communities become more resilient in the face of these challenges.

- **Developing Youth Ambassadors for Arctic Public Outreach and Education Efforts.** The Arctic Youth Ambassadors Program, established by the U.S. Fish and Wildlife Service within the Department of Interior and U.S. Department of State in partnership with nonprofit partner Alaska Geographic, brings together diverse youth from across Alaska to serve as ambassadors for their communities and country to build awareness at home and abroad about life in the Arctic. Over the course of two years, which coincide with the U.S. Chairmanship of the Arctic Council, youth ambassadors are sharing their local perspective on Arctic issues and new knowledge they are gaining by engaging with partners from around the world. The ambassadors represent every major Alaska Native culture and have captured attention on a range issues from climate change to cultural survival.

- **Investing in the Future of Native Youth.** In 2016, the Corporation for National and Community Service (CNCS), which administers AmeriCorps, will invest a record $3.5 million in Tribally-sponsored AmeriCorps programming and $1.25 million in education scholarships. Also in 2016, the National Institute of Food and Agriculture within the Department of Agriculture invested nearly $14 million in 34 Tribal Land Grant Institutions.

- **Training Community Change-makers**. In September 2016, the Department of Housing and Urban Development hosted the 2016 National Native Youth Summit. The summit convened 120 Native Youth Ambassadors, ages 14–17, representing 30 Tribes from all six ONAP regions, to encourage and develop the next generation of Native community leaders. Native Youth Ambassadors were joined by senior officials including Secretary Castro, the Principal Deputy Assistant Secretary for Public and Indian Housing and the Deputy Assistant Secretary for Native American Programs. Native Youth Ambassadors met national leaders, examined the history and inner workings of federal government, and shared experiences and perspectives from their communities. They explored the impact of housing on their community, culture, health, education, conservation, and the environment. Throughout the Summit, Native Youth Ambassadors developed Local Empowerment Projects, such as beautification, preservation, and education that they are now implementing in their communities.

- **Fellowships and Internships for Native Youth**. In 2016 and 2015, several Agencies worked to promote opportunities for Native youth, such as:

  o DOI's Office of the Assistant Secretary – Indian Affairs launched the Student Leadership Summer Institute for Native Students in the summer of 2016 and will continue the program in the summer of 2017. The Institute placed Native students in offices across Indian Affairs in headquarters and throughout the country to gain a better understanding of how Indian Affairs carries out its trust responsibilities.

19

o In 2015, USDA announced 7 fellows for the USDA Terra Preta do Indio Tribal Fellowship. The fellowship is designed to bring together Tribal land-grant faculty and staff, USDA program staff, and others to address challenges in the development of a robust research resource to serve Indian Country and to further advance the United States' food security.

o 2015 HHS Pathways Internship Program: HHS' Indian Health Service (IHS) offered paid internships for youth to participate in IHS operated programs across the country. The internship will promote leadership and professional development, mentorship, economic support and improve college and health career readiness.

- **Improved Data Access for Tribes.** To further Tribal self-determination and provide access to critical decision-making data, in 2013 BIE created a Family Education Rights and Privacy Act Agreement (FERPA) allowing Tribes, as authorized representatives, to access student information data at their BIE funded schools. Agreements further our efforts to improve student performance by strengthening information access and data sharing at the Tribal level. BIE signed its first FERPA Agreement with the Navajo Nation on November 12, 2013. BIE data exchange agreements are available to Tribes and Tribal education departments (TEDs) to promote Tribal efforts to evaluate and improve school programs.

- **STEM Promotion for Native Youth.** The Department of Energy partnered with the American Indian Higher Education Consortium and the American Indian Science and Engineering Society in 2012 to bring science, technology, engineering, and mathematics (STEM) research and education funding to Tribal colleges and universities. This program paired and funded three student/faculty teams from six schools to bring energy projects to Tribal land. The teams were the Navajo Technical College and Arizona State University, the Little Big Horn College and Montana State University, and the Sinte Gleska University and the South Dakota School of Mines and Technology. The teams focused on a wide range of issues, such as solar power for homes, carbon capture, and oil and gas development.

Infrastructure, Economic and Energy Development

In the Obama Administration, federal agencies recognized that in order to promote and sustain prosperous and resilient Tribal nations, a robust economy, clean energy development, strong infrastructure and access to resources for Tribal businesses were needed. Tribal leaders have voiced strongly that the federal government should maintain and even increase its focus on job creation and workforce development in Indian Country.

- **Renewed emphasis on the U.S. Department of Veterans' Affairs Native American Direct Loan Program.** The Native American Direct Loan program assists eligible American Indian and Alaska Native Veterans in financing, buying, or improving homes by providing a low interest rate, no down payment, no private mortgage insurance, and limited closing costs. As of 2016, there are a total of 96 Memoranda of Understanding (MOU) with Tribes.

- **Sustaining Renewable Energy.** Aug. 17, 2016 the U.S. Department of Energy Office (DOE) of Indian Energy announced the availability of up to $3 million to initiate the development of renewable energy and energy efficiency on Tribal lands. Funds can be used to: Conduct energy options analyses; Establish baseline energy use and efficiency options; Develop energy organizations; Conduct climate resiliency planning; Establish policy, regulations, and codes to reduce energy use or promote energy development; Obtain skills and training related to energy use and development.

- **Building Capacity for Indian Energy Needs.** On July 19, 2016, the DOE Office of Indian Energy announced nearly $7 Million in funding to eight inter-Tribal organizations and Alaska Regional Corporations to develop and build their capacity to provide regional technical assistance. The funding, which will help expand the technical assistance network, is expected to leverage more than $1 million in Tribal cost share funds. These build on the $50 million in DOE funding invested in nearly 200 Tribal energy projects between 2002 and 2015. During that same period, Tribes contributed a total of $45 million in cost sharing to advance their energy projects.

- **Clean Energy and Energy Efficiency.** On March 22, 2016, DOE announced funding for 24 American Indian and Alaska Native communities to deploy clean energy and energy efficiency projects. DOE plans to invest over $9 million in 16 facility- and community-scale energy projects in 24 Tribal communities. As part of the Obama Administration's commitment to partner with Tribal Nations, these projects provide Indian Tribes and Alaska Native villages with clean energy solutions that will save communities money and reduce carbon pollution. DOE's funding is expected to leverage nearly $16 million in cost share under the selected Tribal energy projects.

- **Connecting Communities, Improving Infrastructures.** The Department of Transportation's (DOT) Federal Transit Administration (FTA) Tribal Transit Program is expanding its technical assistance efforts to Tribes receiving funds through the Tribal

Transit Technical Assistance Assessments initiative. The FTA has performed 30 assessments and will continue these efforts.

- **Investing in Start-up Firms in Indian Country.** In FY 2015, The Small Business Administration's (SBA) Office of Native American Affairs provided $400,000 toward the creation or expansion of eight Growth Accelerators in Native American communities.

- **Native American Tourism and Improving Visitor Experience Act (NATIVE).** President Obama signed the NATIVE Act in September 2016, the NATIVE Act is a law that enhances and increases Native American tourism, empowers Native American communities, increases coordination and collaboration between federal tourism assets, and expands heritage and cultural tourism opportunities for Tribes. The WHCNAA Economic Development and Infrastructure Subgroup will begin coordinating federal agencies to assist the Act's intentions that increase economic and community development projects on Tribal lands.

- **Entrepreneur Development.** SBA counseled and trained over 12,500 Native American small business owners. This entrepreneurial training was made possible by SBA's Office of Native American Affairs initiative, which provides support to SBA field offices throughout the United States. SBA's four priorities include: (1) increasing knowledge; (2) expanding the capacity and overall development of hosting organizations; (3) strengthening existing and new relationships throughout Indian Country; and (4) increasing knowledge of entrepreneurship programs, and growing the capacity of Native-owned businesses. Over 400 participants received small business development training during 23 events extending across sixteen states. Participants estimated they would create 499 full-time jobs and 205 part-time jobs throughout the country.

- **Investing in Rural Development.** Rural Development within the U.S. Department of Agriculture invested over $3.4 billion dollars in Tribal housing, Tribal infrastructure, Tribal economic development, and Tribal utility development during the Obama Administration. This represents a marked increase in the pace of investment as in the preceding 8 fiscal years when $1.7 billion was invested in Indian Country and Alaska through the same programs. USDA Rural Development's loan and grant programs helped finance new Tribal school and Tribal College facilities, broadband infrastructure, medical facilities, entrepreneurial opportunities, Tribal economic development enterprises and new and rehabilitated housing options.

Health and Wellness in Indian Country

Over the past eight years, the federal government has sought to reinforce its treaty and trust obligations for healthcare to American Indian and Alaska Natives by securing permanent healthcare funding, striving to reduce chronic disease and childhood obesity, and focusing on behavioral health issues such as suicide and trauma.

Historic gains in health and wellness for Indian Country were achieved in 2010 by the passage of the Affordable Care Act (ACA) which includes permanent reauthorization of the Indian Health Care Improvement Act (IHCIA).

As part of this Administration's efforts to break down siloes among federal partners, the Department of Health and Human Services (HHS) and the Department of Veteran's Affairs (VA) have coordinated to securely share health information to improve services to Tribal patients, and the Department of Housing and Urban Development (HUD) and the VA have collaborated to tackle homelessness for Tribal veterans. Lastly, American Indian and Alaska Native patients now have an office devoted solely to behavioral and mental health issues, the Office of Tribal Affairs and Policy in HHS' Substance Abuse and Mental Health Services Administration (SAMHSA) that regularly teams up with the Departments of Justice (DOJ) and Interior (DOI) on inter-agency work.

- **Commission on Native Children.** In 2016, President Obama signed the Alyce Spotted Bear and Walter Soboleff Commission on Native Children Act. The Act calls for the creation of a Commission on Native Children that will conduct a comprehensive study of Federal, State, local, and Tribal programs that serve Native children. The Commission's study will develop recommendations for Federal policy relating to Native children, including, but not limited to, improvements to the child welfare system, increased access to mental and physical health care, improvements to educational and vocational opportunities, and more flexible use of existing Federal programs that serve Native populations. The Commission will submit a detailed report on the findings of its study to the President and Congress.

- **Responding to Behavioral Health Issues.** In response to the high rates of mental and substance use disorders among American Indians and Alaska Natives, within HHS, SAMHSA created the Office of Tribal Affairs and Policy (OTAP) in 2014. OTAP serves as the agency point of contact for Tribal governments, Tribal organizations, federal departments' and agencies' Tribal affairs efforts, and other governments and agencies on behavioral health issues facing American Indians and Alaska Natives. The office brings together SAMHSA's Tribal affairs, Tribal policy, Tribal consultation, Tribal advisory, and requirements of Tribal Law and Order Act (TLOA) of 2010.

In FY 2014, SAMHSA awarded more than $61 million in total funding over five years for behavioral health services for Native youth to promote prevention, treatment, and recovery from mental and substance use disorders. The funding was supported through multiple SAMHSA programs including, Circles of Care, State/Tribal Youth Suicide Prevention, the Tribal Behavioral Health Grant program (also known as Native Connections), Partnerships for Success State and Tribal Initiative, and SAMHSA Adult Tribal Healing to Wellness Courts and Juvenile Treatment Drug Courts. The Tribal Behavioral Health Grant program was established in FY 2014 and focuses on preventing and reducing suicidal behavior and substance misuse and promoting mental health among American Indian and Alaska Native young people up to and including age 24. The program allows Tribes and Tribal organizations maximum flexibility to plan and implement programs that best meet community needs.

In November 2014, SAMHSA hosted its first cross-agency Tribal conference focused on improving behavioral health outcomes for Native youth. The conference sought to: increase awareness about behavioral health issues and building skills; provide a platform for the Native youth voice; engage and connect Native youth in a continuing national dialogue about behavioral health; and promote best and promising practices. More than 225 youth and adults representing approximately 70 Tribes and Tribal organizations participated in the conference.

- **Addressing Suicidal Behavior in Tribal communities.** In FY 2016, SAMHSA released two reports focused on addressing suicide in Tribal communities. The first report, *Preventing and Responding to Suicide Clusters in American Indian and Alaska Native Communities*, provides information about events and responses within two Tribal communities that experienced youth suicide clusters as a means for informing future responses. The second report, *Suicide Prevention in Alaska*, informs Tribal communities, policymakers, and public health professionals about suicide prevention efforts in Alaskan villages with recommendations for action.

In FY 2016, funding for the Tribal Behavioral Health Grant (TBHG) program, which supports Generation Indigenous Initiative awarded grants to 70 new Tribes and Tribal organizations to prevent and reduce suicidal behavior and substance misuse and promote mental health among American Indian and Alaska Native young people. This second cohort of the TBHG program more explicitly supports Tribal efforts to address trauma in their communities. Over the course of five years the programs is estimated to invest approximately $95 million in Tribal behavioral health.

- **Addressing Alcohol and Substance Abuse.** SAMHSA established the Office of Indian Alcohol and Substance Abuse (OIASA) in response to the Tribal Law and Order Act (TLOA) of 2010. OIASA is a component of SAMHSA's Office of Tribal Affairs and Policy and leads activities in collaboration with the Indian Health Service (IHS), DOI's Bureau of Indian Affairs and Bureau of Indian Education, and DOJ. In 2016, the Secretary of HHS, the Attorney General, and the Secretary of DOI signed a new Memorandum of Agreement to further collaborative alcohol and substance abuse activities.

- **National Tribal Behavioral Health Agenda (TBHA).** In December 2016, HHS launched the National Tribal Behavioral Health Agenda (TBHA). This first Tribal-federal blueprint responds to a call by Tribal leaders for improved collaboration with federal agencies who hold responsibility for addressing and/or responding to the impacts of mental and substance use disorders. The TBHA was developed based on extensive Tribal input and was led by the SAMHSA and IHS in collaboration with the National Indian Health Board. The TBHA includes an American Indian and Alaska Native Cultural Wisdom Declaration which acknowledges that cultural wisdom and traditional practices are fundamental to achieving behavioral health improvements today and to affect change for future generations. The TBHA focuses on:
  o Healing from historical and intergenerational trauma
  o Facilitating a socio-cultural-ecological approach for improving behavioral health
  o Increasing prevention and recovery supports
  o Improving behavioral health systems and services
  o Raising awareness of behavioral health conditions related to Tribal communities
  o Recognizing and supporting integration of cultural wisdom and traditional practices
  o into behavioral health programs and services
  o Strategies to address and reduce behavioral health issues

- **Data Sharing Capability.** In 2015, IHS and the VA became the first federal agencies to gain accreditation in interoperability, allowing improvements in health data exchange and health care coordination for Native American veterans.

- **The Tiwahe Initiative.** The Tiwahe is a five-year demonstration project that began in FY 2015. Tiwahe (ti-wah-hay) means family in the Lakota language. The overall goal of the Initiative is to improve the health, safety, and well-being of families by implementation of a coordinated service delivery model among Tribal agencies and justice systems to: increase access to family and social services; create alternatives to incarceration via culturally- and solution-focused sentencing options; improve links to appropriate prevention, intervention, and treatment opportunities; improve case management services; and improve the overall partnership among local, Tribal, county, state, and federal providers to increase access to services for Tribal children, youth and families. There are a total of six Tiwahe demonstration sites across Indian Country at present.

- **IHS and Tribal Health Program Reimbursement Agreements.** The VA-IHS MOU authorized the creation of reimbursement agreements to enable VA to reimburse IHS and Tribally operated health programs for direct care services provided to eligible American Indian and Alaska Native Veterans. A national reimbursement agreement was signed between VA and IHS in 2012. An implementation plan is used to set up reimbursement processes at each IHS site. As implementation plans are rolled out to more IHS sites, more reimbursements can occur under the National Reimbursement Agreement. Tribal health programs enter into local reimbursement agreements with nearby VA Medical Centers. As of 2016, there are a total of 95 signed local reimbursement agreements with Tribal health programs totaling $45 million in reimbursements.

- **Tribal HUD-VA Supported Housing Demonstration Program.** Approximately 2.6 percent of the standard HUD-VA Supported Housing program (HUD-VASH) serves Native American or Alaska Native Veterans who are living outside of Tribal trust lands. HUD and VA are collaboratively implementing a Tribal HUD-VASH demonstration program targeting Native American Veterans who are homeless or at risk of homelessness and live on or near Tribal trust land. This program provides approximately 500 units of tenant and projected based rental assistance to 26 Tribes.

- **Supporting Traditional Foods in Indian Country.** The Agricultural Act of 2014, better known as the 2014 Farm Bill, provided additional flexibility for the U.S. Department of Agriculture (USDA) to incorporate traditional foods into the Food Distribution Program on Indian Reservations (FDPIR) program. In 2016, USDA increased the quantity and variety of traditional foods being distributed to low-income families and the elderly. In 2016, USDA established the Tribal Leaders Working Group on the Food Distribution Program for Indian Reservations (FDPIR) to focus on processes to support a better program for Tribal participants.

Public Safety and Justice

Tribal governments, like any government, have responsibilities to their citizens to preserve public safety and to maintain effective justice systems. Due to the complex nature of Tribal jurisdiction created by federal statutes and federal court decisions, Tribes often face unique challenges with policing and maintaining public safety. The Administration has worked with Tribes and Congress over the past eight years to address these challenges.

President Obama signed into law milestone legislation with the Violence Against Women Reauthorization Act of 2013 (VAWA) and the Tribal Law and Order Act of 2010 (TLOA), steadily strengthening the federal government's commitment to Tribal self-governance. Recognizing that local policing is more effective for Tribal communities, TLOA authorizes enhanced authority for Tribes to prosecute and punish criminals. In response to the disproportionate rate of abuse for Native women, VAWA authorizes Tribes to exercise their sovereign power to investigate, prosecute, convict, and sentence both Indian and non-Indians who assault Indian spouses or dating partners within Indian country. The Administration is also engaged with Canada and Mexico on violence against indigenous women.

- **National Indian Country Training Initiative.** In July 2010, the Department of Justice (DOJ) launched the National Indian Country Training Initiative (NICTI) to ensure that Department prosecutors, as well as state and Tribal criminal justice personnel, receive the training and support needed to address the particular challenges relevant to Indian country prosecutions. This training effort is led by the Department's National Indian Country Training Coordinator and is based at the National Advocacy Center (NAC) in Columbia, SC. The NICTI will train approximately 2,500 criminal justice and social service personnel in FY 16.

- **Tribal Court Trial Advocacy Training.** Starting in 2011, at the Department of Interior DOI's), the Bureau of Indian Affairs' Office of Tribal Justice Support, with the support of DOJ's Office for Access to Justice (ATJ), launched the Tribal Court Trial Advocacy Training program. This three-day trial advocacy course is designed to improve the trial skills of judges, public defenders, and prosecutors who appear in Tribal courts. Trainings are free and are staffed by attorneys from ATJ, Assistant United States Attorneys who practice in Indian Country, the Executive Office for U.S. Attorneys' Native American Issues Coordinator, Assistant Federal Public Defenders, and Tribal prosecutors, public defenders, and judges.

- **Attorney General's Task Force on American Indian and Alaska Native Children Exposed to Violence.** In 2013, then-Attorney General Eric Holder announced the creation of the Attorney General's Task Force on American Indian and Alaska Native Children Exposed to Violence. The Task Force was created in response to a recommendation in the Attorney General's National Task Force on Children Exposed to Violence December 2012 final report which noted that American Indian and Alaska Native children have an exceptional degree of unmet needs for services and support to prevent and respond to the extreme levels of violence they experience. The Task Force was anchored by both a federal working group and an advisory committee of experts appointed to examine the scope and impact of violence facing American Indian and Alaska Native children and make policy recommendations to the Attorney General on ways to address it. Based on the testimony at four public hearings, comprehensive research, and extensive input from experts, advocates, and impacted families and communities nationwide, the Advisory Committee on American Indian Alaska Native Children Exposed to Violence issued a final report to the Attorney General presenting its findings and comprehensive policy recommendations in November 2014. The report serves as a blueprint for preventing children's exposure to violence and for reducing the negative effects experienced by children exposed to violence across the United States.

- **Coordinated Tribal Assistance Solicitation.** Through a Coordinated Tribal Assistance Solicitation the DOJ has awarded over 1,600 grants totaling more than $722 million to hundreds of American Indian and Alaska Native communities. The Tribes are using these funds to enhance law enforcement, bolster justice systems, prevent and control delinquency, strengthen the juvenile justice system, serve sexual assault and elder victims, and support other efforts to combat crime.

- **North American Working Group on Violence against Indigenous Women and Girls.** In October 2016, he United States, Canada, and Mexico committed to improve coordination on violence against Indigenous women and girls. On June 29, 2016, President Obama met with Prime Minister Justin Trudeau of Canada and President Enrique Peña Nieto of Mexico. The three presidents made a tri-lateral commitment to address the scourge of violence against indigenous women and girls that exists across North America. A working group, involving the Attorney General and leaders from Canada and Mexico was established as a result of that tri-lateral commitment. The first working group meeting was held with the Attorneys General from all three nations in October 2016.

- **Responding to Sexual Assault.** On June 27, 2016, Attorney General Lynch issued a directive requiring United States Attorneys with jurisdiction to prosecute crimes in Indian Country to meet with federal (Federal Bureau of Investigation Bureau of Indian Affairs and Indian Health Service) and Tribal partners to develop written sexual violence guidelines that detail specific responsibilities of each federal partner in responding to sexual violence in Indian country. The recommendations were based on a final report that was issued by the National Coordination Committee of the American Indian / Alaska Native Sexual Assault Nurse Examiner-Sexual Assault Response Team (SANE/SART) Initiative in 2014. All USAOs have submitted their guidelines to EOUSA.

- **Tribal Law and Order Act.** The Tribal Law and Order Act (TLOA) of 2010 fills key gaps in our criminal justice system. TLOA seeks to address challenges faced in Tribal justice systems, to establish greater accountability for federal agencies responsible for prosecuting crime on reservations, and to provide Tribes with the tools to combat extremely high rates of crime. In signing the bill, President Obama remarked that it is "unconscionable that crime rates in Indian Country are more than twice the national average and up to 20 times the national average on some reservations."

  DOJ published a final rule in December 2011 implementing Section 221 of the TLOA, which authorizes the Attorney General to assume concurrent jurisdiction over crimes committed on certain Tribal lands. Through this rule, an Indian tribe that is subject to Public Law 280 may request that the federal government accept concurrent jurisdiction within the tribe's territory and, if the Attorney General consents, federal authorities can investigate and prosecute criminal offenses. Several Tribes have submitted requests for assumption by the Attorney General of concurrent federal criminal jurisdiction, all of which have been resolved.

- **Tribal Access Program for National Crime Information.** DOJ launched the Tribal Access Program for National Crime Information (TAP) in August 2015 to provide Tribes access to national crime information systems for both civil and criminal purposes. TAP allows Tribes to more effectively serve and protect their nation's citizens by ensuring the exchange of critical data across the Criminal Justice Information Services systems and other national crime information systems. In 2015, DOJ selected Tribes to participate in the initial User Feedback Phase. This partnership focused on testing DOJ's technology solution and training support; it also enabled Tribes to identify and share best practices regarding the use of national crime information databases to strengthen public safety. In 2016, participating Tribes received a kiosk workstation that provided access to national systems as well as training to support whole-of-government needs. User Feedback Phase Tribes have elected to implement TAP in a variety of criminal and civil agencies. DOJ plans to expand this program in 2017.

Environment, Climate Change, and Natural Resources

Beginning with the President's first term, Tribes have repeatedly expressed their concerns for a healthy and resilient natural environment. Tribal leaders, particularly Alaska Native leaders, have shared dire examples of villages and communities facing the impacts of climate change, including significantly diminished wild game and fish, unprecedented erosion, rising sea levels, and thawing permafrost. These events have direct impacts on the livelihood and culture of Tribes.

- **Climate Resilience Toolkit.** The Department of Interior (DOI), Environmental Protection Agency (EPA), and other federal agencies created the online Climate Resilience Toolkit, which compiles and organizes resources to assist Tribes in climate-change planning, adaptation, and mitigation. The agencies developed grants for direct support for Tribal planning, vulnerability assessments, and support from Tribal climate scientists. Many agencies made strides to incorporate traditional Tribal knowledge into their programs and assessments.

- **State, Local and Tribal Leaders Task Force on Climate Preparedness and Resilience, Tribal Supplemental Recommendations Progress Report.** This 2016 report identifies programs and policies that Federal agencies have developed or updated in response to the Tribal Supplemental Recommendations, which focus on the specific and unique perspectives of Native communities to build resilience to the impacts of climate change.

- **Cleanup of Environmental Contamination in Indian Country.** In *Tronox, Incorporated v. Anadarko Petroleum Corp.*, the United States obtained a $5.15 billion settlement related to the environmental liabilities of the historic Kerr-McGee Corporation, including $985 million to fund the cleanup of approximately 50 abandoned uranium mines in and around the Navajo Nation, where radioactive waste remains from Kerr-McGee mining operations.

- **Engaging Communities to Connect with Technical Experts through Community Based Data Collection.** EPA's Indian Environmental General Assistance Program provided a grant to the Alaska Native Tribal Health Consortium, to support the release of a Local Environmental Observer (LEO) Mobile Application (App). Expanding on the successful computer-based tool, the App allows observers to share photos and text from the field, complete with GPS locations to allow communities to monitor, respond to, and adapt to new impacts and health effects.

- **Federal-Tribal Climate Resilience Partnership.** In 2014, DOI's Bureau of Indian Affairs Office of Trust Services in coordination with DOI and the White House announced funding to address climate Resilience in Indian Country and Alaska Native Villages. The Federal-Tribal Climate Resilience Partnership and Technical Assistance Program included grants for direct support of Tribal planning, vulnerability assessments, monitoring, and ocean and coastal planning in concert with technical support in the form of Tribal climate scientists collocated in five climate science service centers.

- **Environmental Justice Policy.** In July 2014, EPA issued its policy on Environmental Justice for Working with Federally Recognized Tribes and Indigenous Peoples. The Policy is designed to clarify and better integrate environmental justice principles in a consistent manner in EPA's work with federally recognized Tribes and indigenous peoples, such as when matters of environmental justice are brought to the attention of EPA. Over the three-year policy development process, the EPA hosted Tribal consultations, public comment engagements, and numerous meetings with Tribal leaders and indigenous organizations.

- **National Climate Assessment.** In 2013, the U.S. Geological Survey (USGS) within DOI led an effort to ensure that the National Climate Assessment reports included Tribal lands and communities for the very first time, with a comprehensive review of the impacts and adaptation efforts of Tribes in the Southwest. This work, as well as other USGS research, helped raise awareness regarding the contributions of traditional knowledge to understanding climate change impacts in regions of the United States outside Alaska. Continuing work on the impact of climate change to Tribes in the Southwestern United States includes an examination of increasing temperatures on drought impacts, their effects on Navajo rangeland, and possible management strategies to mitigate these impacts.

  The USGS National Climate Change and Wildlife Science Center convened the initial meeting of a Tribal and Indigenous Knowledge Working Group, under the auspices of the newly established Advisory Committee on Climate Change and Natural Resource Science (ACCCNRS). The Group, which contains Tribal representation, is developing a work plan for Tribal/indigenous matters for ACCCNRS, focusing initially on Tribal climate science needs, effective communication between Federal climate science efforts and Tribes, capacity gaps in Indian country, and traditional/local ecological knowledge.

- **Toxics Release Inventory Program.** In April 2012, EPA issued a rule that provides Tribal governments with more opportunities to fully participate in the Toxic Release Inventory (TRI) Program. The rule is part of the EPA's ongoing efforts to increase Tribal participation in the TRI Program and improve Tribal access to information on toxic chemical releases that affect Tribal communities.

31

- **Protecting Air Quality with New Source Review Rules.** EPA issued New Source Review rules to bring regulatory parity and certainty to sources (entities that have the potential to emit pollutants) in or considering locating in Indian Country. EPA also finalized a guidance for Tribes on participating in the process for designating areas as 'attainment' or 'non-attainment' areas for ground-level ozone standards created in 2015 and to recognize Tribal jurisdiction and boundaries.

- **National Ocean Policy.** On July 19, 2010, President Obama established the National Ocean Policy through Executive Order 13547—*Stewardship of the Ocean, Our Coasts, and the Great Lakes*. To improve coordination and collaboration, and to ensure the participation of Tribal, State, and local officials in National Ocean Policy activities, the Executive Order also established a Governance Coordinating Committee (GCC) consisting of 18 members, three of whom are Tribal representatives. The National Ocean Policy calls for the inclusion of Tribal authorities, among others, in collaborative, regional marine planning activities.

- **Drought Response.** In 2016, the U. S. Bureau of Reclamation (Reclamation) at DOI provided approximately $7 million to assist Tribes in addressing the impacts of severe drought affecting Indian Tribes in California, Colorado, Idaho, New Mexico, Nevada, Oklahoma, and South Dakota. The projects assisted Tribes in developing comprehensive drought response plans and improving existing water facilities to support conservation and efficiency. As a result, Reclamation has helped Tribes strengthen their ability to provide essential water supplies and manage their water resources in a sustainable manner. In addition, Reclamation provided approximately $2 million in technical assistance grants to assist Tribes to develop, maintain and protect their water and related resources.

Respecting Tribal Sovereignty, Knowledge, and Culture

By acknowledging in federal processes and decision-making the sophisticated and unique knowledge Tribes have about their lands, natural resources, and citizens, the federal government can better meet the trust responsibility it has to Tribes. Working closely with Tribes and respecting Tribal culture helps ensure that agency actions, policies, and laws are implemented capably in Tribal communities. Over the course of the Obama Administration, the federal government has worked to protect the cultural rights and sacred sites of Tribes for generations to come. Federal Departments have recognized the practical use of Tribes managing or co-managing land and natural and cultural resources. By respecting and supporting Tribal sovereignty, the health of the federal-Tribal relationship continues to be restored.

- **Contract Support Costs.** The Department of the Interior (DOI) settled a long-standing litigation related to funding contract support costs for self-governance compacts. Full funding of these costs is necessary to ensure successful implementation of federal programs assumed by participating Tribes, a key factor in furthering self-determination and self-governance.

- **Educating federal staff about sacred sites.** In 2016, the U.S. Department of Agriculture's Forest Service (USDA Forest Service) developed national training curriculum to engage employees in protecting sacred places and conducted two pilot trainings. The USDA Forest Service also conducted a series of five national-level webinars to present and discuss efforts that protected sacred places on National Forests and Grasslands.

- **Mapping tools.** The USDA Forest Service developed the web-based GIS map service Tribal Connections that illustrates relationships between federal public lands, Indian trust lands, and lands ceded by Tribes through treaties. The USDA Forest Service also sponsored the book *Native Americans and National Forests, an administrative history of the relationships between Tribes and the Forest Service.*

- **Tribally-Supporting Research.** In 2015, The USDA Forest Service published the Research and Development Tribal Research Roadmap, which lays out a strategic approach to involving Tribes in Forest Service Research and Development activities. (2016) The USDA Forest Service published the follow up document, Research and Development Tribal Research Roadmap Highlights Report to tell the stories behind 27 local and landscape-scale engagements of Tribal interest.

- **Protecting Cultural Landscapes and Sacred Places.** The Departments of Defense, Interior, Agriculture and Energy and the Advisory Council on Historic Preservation (ACHP) renewed, for an additional five years, a Memorandum of Understanding regarding interagency coordination and collaboration for the protection of Indian sacred sites.

- **Supporting Self Determination in the Protection of Historic Properties.** The National Historic Preservation Act includes a provision for the ACHP to enter into agreements with Indian Tribes to substitute a tribe's historic preservation regulations for the ACHP's regulations, commonly called the Section 106 process. Under such an arrangement, an Indian tribe has the ability to determine how federal agencies meet the requirements of Section 106 for projects on its lands. To both encourage Tribes to consider such arrangements and to help them navigate the decision making process, the ACHP, in consultation with Indian Tribes, will issue formal guidance in 2017.

- **DOI Cooperative Management.** DOI heard from many Tribes, especially in Alaska, about the need for cooperative management of federal land between Tribes and the United States. Secretary Jewell responded to this input by issuing Secretarial Order 3342. The Order encourages cooperative management agreements between DOI and Tribes and establishes a process and institutional support to ensure that cooperative management opportunities are developed. Additionally, the Order recognizes that Tribes have traditional ecological knowledge and practices that can assist Federal management decision making. Since the Order was issued, DOI signed an agreement with the Ahtna Intertribal Resource Commission to create a wildlife management demonstration project in Southcentral Alaska.

- **Federal Subsistence Board.** The interagency Federal Subsistence Board comprises five Federal agency seats, including the Alaska State Director of the Bureau of Land Management, the USDA Forest Service Alaska Regional Forester, and the Alaska Regional Directors of the Bureau of Indian Affairs, National Park Service, and the U.S. Fish and Wildlife Service within DOI. The Board also includes three public members, the chair and two rural subsistence user seats, appointed by the Secretary of the Interior with the concurrence of the Secretary of Agriculture. The Board published its Tribal Consultation Policy in recognition of the unique role that the subsistence way of life sustains health, life, safety, and cultures of Alaska Native peoples, as it has done since time immemorial.

- **Updates to Federal Acknowledgement of Indian Tribes.** DOI finalized reforms to the regulatory process by which DOI officially recognizes Indian Tribes (25 CFR Part 83). July 30, DOI finalized new rule establishing procedures for the new administrative hearing on federal acknowledgement (43 CFR Part 4 subpart k). The updated rules promote a more transparent, timely, and consistent process that is flexible enough to account for the unique histories of Tribal communities, while maintaining the rigor and integrity of the criteria that have been in place for nearly 40 years. The updated rules implement DOI's authority to recognize those Tribes that have maintained their identity and self-governance in the face of significant and longstanding challenges.

- **Native American Graves Protection and Repatriation Act.** In 2015, DOI issued a final rule implementing section 3(b) of the Native American Graves Protection and Repatriation Act (NAGPRA) a milestone in signifying the Administration's respect for the cultural rights of Tribal nations. The final rule provides procedures for the disposition of unclaimed human remains, funerary objects, sacred objects, or objects of cultural patrimony excavated or discovered on, and removed from, federal lands after November 16, 1990.

- **HEARTH Act.** On July 30, 2012, President Obama signed the Helping Expedite and Advance Responsible Tribal Homeownership Act (HEARTH Act) and updated regulations pertaining to leasing Tribal lands and issuing rights-of-way over Tribal land into law. This new law restores the authority of Indian Tribes to control the leasing of Tribal lands.

  In November 2012, DOI published final revisions to its regulations governing the leasing of Indian lands. These revisions mark the most significant changes to DOI's Indian leasing regulations in 50 years and will reduce the timelines for the Bureau of Indian Affairs (BIA) to review and approve leases. Additionally, DOI announced a new categorical exclusion for leases of Indian lands for single-family homes on August 10, 2012. This is the BIA's first new categorical exclusion in more than a decade, and in April 2016, the Administration's updated the rights-of-way regulations became effective. The updated regulations streamline the process for obtaining BIA approval, ensure consistency with the updated leasing regulations, and increase flexibility in compensation and valuations, and support landowner decisions regarding use of their land.

- **United Nations Declaration on Rights on the Indigenous Peoples (Declaration).** In 2010, President Obama announced that the United States supports the United Nations Declaration on the Rights of Indigenous Peoples (Declaration). As President Obama made clear; "What matters far more than words—what matters far more than any resolution or declaration—are actions to match those words." Other significant United Nations-related work that followed included:
  o (2011) United States first-ever report to the United Nations Human Rights Council under the Universal Periodic Review Process.
  o (2013) The ACHP adopted a plan to support the Declaration and remains committed to raising awareness about the Declaration throughout the preservation community and to incorporate its principles and aspirations into all of its work.
  o (2014) United States advocacy for indigenous rights at the World Conference on Indigenous Peoples, as led by the first-ever Native American United States ambassador, Keith Harper, Ambassador to the Human Rights Council.
  o (2014) United States reporting on compliance with the International Covenant on Civil and Political Rights
  o (2014) United States reporting on compliance with the Convention on the
  o Elimination of All Forms of Racial Discrimination.
  o (2015) United States second reporting to the United Nations Human Rights Council under the Universal Periodic Review Process.
  o (2016) United States advocacy for direct indigenous government participation in

- o United Nations processes and enhancement of the Expert Mechanism on the Rights of Indigenous Peoples to afford better assessment of the protection of indigenous rights.
- o (2016) DOI and the Environmental Protection Agency and jointly commenced an effort to develop training for domestic implementation of the United Declaration on the Rights of Indigenous Peoples pursuant to the Executive Order 12898, Federal Actions to Address Environmental Justice in Minority and Low-Income Populations, and in furtherance of the Universal Periodic Review Process.
- o (2016) Consultation on ways for the United States to assist Tribes in their efforts repatriate Tribal cultural heritage from foreign auction sales and foreign museum holding

White House Council on Native American Affairs

Prosperity and resilience for all Tribal nations is the vision of the White House Council on Native American Affairs (WHCNAA). The WHCNAA endeavors toward this vision through collaborative inter-agency work across the Executive Branch, by fostering an *all-of-government* approach in meeting treaty and trust obligations to Tribes. Beginning with the President's first term, Tribal leaders underscored the need for a Cabinet-level council to uphold the unique nation-to-nation relationship with Tribal nations. The formation of the WHCHAA directly responds to those Tribal leader recommendations.

Chaired by the Secretary of the Interior, WHCNAA membership consists of heads of federal Departments, Agencies, and Offices, with an Executive Director and inter-agency staff carrying forward WHCNAA priorities. The priorities revolve, generally, around Tribal self-determination and Tribal self-governance. Consistent and substantive engagement between the WHCNAA and Tribal leaders sets the foundation for effective federal investments in Tribal communities and for effective policies that impact Tribes. Many instances exist for WHCNAA dialogue with Tribal leaders, such as the WHCNAA principals meetings and through WHCNAA subgroups.

WHCNAA Chair Secretary Jewell set the precedent for Tribal leader attendance and participation at the principals meetings, which occur three times per year. Tribal leader attendance at the principals meetings is coordinated through the WHCNAA six subgroups. The subgroups produce deliverables and tools, make policy recommendations, and find ways to leverage resources and expertise among agencies to improve services to Indian Country. The subgroups meet regularly and provide reports at each of the WHCNAA principals meetings.

Improved and Sustained Federal Actions in Indian Country

The milestones shared by Tribal nations and the Administration over the past eight years set a strong foundation for continued mutual progress well beyond the Obama Administration. The momentum from years of hard work and regular nation-to-nation dialogue must be carried forward to address issues that need renewed focus and resources for Tribal communities. The WHCNAA offers Indian Country – and the federal government – an organizational structure to respond to the numerous matters that require inter-agency attention.

Tribal leaders have shared their priorities at each of the White House Tribal Nations Conferences. In moving forward, the WHCNAA subgroups will address as many of those as feasible. For long-term, positive impacts on many of the priorities, like improving access to data and job/workforce development, an all-of-government approach must be pursued. Agencies must seek to leverage and coordinate their programs and expertise with other agencies, strategically.

Economic Development & Infrastructure Subgroup

The U.S. Department of Agriculture (USDA) and the Small Business Administration (SBA) co-lead the subgroup with participation from Treasury, HUD, Commerce, Transportation, Labor, DOE, DOI, and others. The subgroup creates, improves, and promotes opportunities for economic development for Tribes and American Indian and Alaska Native (AI/AN). The subgroup also works across agencies to address wide-ranging aspects of improving infrastructure in Indian Country It promotes existing federal programs that support economic development and explores new investment models for Tribes via specific financing options.

The subgroup has worked to improve financial education in Indian Country, organize resources for housing and community development, increase exposure to apprenticeship opportunities, and explore ways to streamline resources for feasibility studies and improving technical capacity for Tribes.

Moving forward, the subgroup will continue focusing on efforts to improve job/workforce development, the economic possibilities presented by the recently passed NATIVE Act, and Tribal engagement.

Health Subgroup

The Health and Wellness subgroup is being led by Health and Human Services and was established in response to feedback from Tribal leaders. The goal of the subgroup is improved interagency collaboration and coordination to prevent health problems and address health issues to strengthen Native families and support Tribal communities.

In FY 2016, the Health Subgroup developed a proposal for a multi-departmental initiative to address the impacts of trauma in Tribal communities. The symptoms and long-term effects of historical trauma include psychological distress, poor overall physical and mental health, and unmet medical and psychological needs evidenced by increased exposure to trauma, depressive symptoms, substance use, and suicidal thoughts and attempts. Traumatic events that undermine the culture and identity of Indian peoples disrupt not only individual lives, but also a community's capacity to regroup or rebuild in healthful way.

The Health Subgroup proposal is focused on federal agencies who are working to support their agencies' efforts with Tribes. The proposal includes three prongs:
1) Increase awareness and understanding of trauma.
2) Improve coordination and collaboration.
3) Build federal capacity through technical assistance

Education & Native Youth Subgroup

The Education and Native Youth subgroup with the co-leads of Department of the Interior and the Department of Education focused early attention to the reform of the Bureau of Indian Education. The White House Initiative on American Indian and Alaska Native Education, which is housed in the Department of Education, leads initiatives relating to Native Youth Community Projects and Native language rejuvenation efforts in schools.

Additionally, as part of this subgroup Health and Human Services is leading work to continue and sustain the Generation Indigenous (Gen-I) program. The Education & Native Youth subgroup will continue work on efforts underway and set new goals and priorities in response to Tribal leader input received during the 2016 White House Tribal Leaders Conference.

Energy Subgroup

The Energy subgroup with co-leads of the Department of Energy and the Department of the Interior works to identify areas where federal agencies can collaborate to support Tribal energy development, including financial and technical assistance programs, workforce development, regulatory streamlining, federal procurement, and project support. The subgroup prioritized information for Indian Tribes through an online tool called the "Federal Grant, Loan, and Technical Assistance Programs for Tribal Energy Development".

The online tool provides a centralized repository of federal funding and technical assistance programs and information about the major energy, energy infrastructure, economic development, and environmental programs and regulations that support energy development and deployment in Indian Country and Alaska Native villages.

Environment, Climate Change, and Natural Resources Subgroup

The Environment, Climate Change, and Natural Resources subgroup, with co-leads of the Department of the Interior and the Environmental Protection Agency, focus on protecting natural environments for Tribal communities, including mitigation efforts against the devastating effects of climate change for some Tribes, and the protection and management of natural resources for Tribes.

The subgroup has developed Federal Tribal Climate Change Resource Guide that links to partners, tools, opportunities, funding, products, and services available to Tribes to support climate adaptation planning and mitigation. The guide has participation from federal partners, including National Aeronautics and Space Administration, National Oceanic and Atmospheric Administration, Department of Energy Department of Defense Center for Disease Control U.S. Department of Agriculture, Environmental Protection Agency, and several Department of Interior bureaus, and custom Tribal pages.

The subgroup has advanced local science-based approaches to combating climate change, through efforts like the Local Environmental Observers (LEO) Network, which is a network of local observers and topic experts who share knowledge about unusual animal, environment, and weather events. With LEO, users can connect with others in their community, share observations, raise awareness, and find answers about significant environmental events. Users can also engage with topic experts in many different organizations and become part of a broader observer community.

Lastly, nine Cabinet members and heads of offices signed an interagency MOU on the protection of Tribal treaty rights on natural resources in federal decision-making. A working group has formed from this MOU to further the MOU's implementation.

Public Safety & Justice Subgroup

The Department of Justice and Department of the Interior co-chair the Public Safety and Justice subgroup. The Departments formed the subgroup in response to the needs expressed by Tribal leaders for the WHCNAA to concentrate on the unique legal and public safety concerns facing Indian Country, such as jurisdictional matters, violence in Indian Country, infrastructure, training and capacity for Tribal police and judicial systems, and more.

The subgroup assembles other critical agencies and leverages collective knowledge and resources of subgroup members, approaching public safety issues from an inter-agency perspective. The subgroup will also ensure that input from Tribal representatives informs the identification and treatment of issues under consideration, such as violence against women and girls in Tribal communities, curbing recidivism, and strengthening Tribal policing capacity.